Content

Testimonials

"Cody makes it simple. I love it." – **Sarah, independent investor, 2011**

"Cody Willard, is one of the best Wall Street analysts in the business....and he has the best hair on Wall Street." – **Jay Leno, 2008**

"What I love about Cody, is, I can understand everything he tells us. When all these investor sites start using their industry jargon, I am totally lost, understanding about 1/3 of what they are talking about. They aren't lawyers, after all, can't they just speak in a language most of us understand?" – **Alice, independent investor, 2012**

"Cody Willard has been on top of it. If you want to know more about trading this stuff, you want to read what he has to say." – **Jim Cramer, legendary hedge fund manager and CNBC anchor, 2005**

"What more could you want? Insightful information and an expert on the technology revolution taking place today." – **Brent, independent investor, 2011**

"Cody Willard, co-host of Fox Business Network's 'Happy Hour,' would hardly be mistaken for a pinstriped Wall Street drone. But he's got some serious financial credentials." – **Los Angeles Times, 2009**

"I'm a member of Cody's newsletter since the days of Cody recommending Apple in the teens and buying Google after the Dutch IPO. Everyone, he's the best!" – **Rohit, independent investor, 2011**

"One of the most independent-minded and insightful dudes in business. Cody's enthusiasm and being right more often than not made me appreciate his approach to making the important calls when all hell is breaking loose." – Diane, independent investor, 2011

"For the past 10 years, every single time I've made a significant tech investment I make one and only one call: to Cody Willard. He is the best tech investor out there." – **James Altucher, Formula Capital CEO, 2011**

"Cody Willard, a Wall Street wonder at 25." – **NY Daily News, 2006**

Introduction

In 1996 I came to New York City with a degree in economics from the University of New Mexico, a suitcase, a guitar and just about nothing else. I dreamed of becoming a "Wall Street Rock Star," so while I was searching for a way to get my foot in the door anywhere I could, I devoured every book on trading, stocks, investing, options, brokering, and economics. None of them really delivered the hard truths along with the information and knowledge base that every investor and trader needs to know.

In the years since, I became the first ever partner of a legendary stock broker and analyst by the name of Andrew Lanyi. I ran the research division at a venture capital tech fund. I ran the wholesale division of a major telecom company. I wrote a technology newsletter for *TheStreet.com* and a long-time investment column for the *Financial Times*. I launched a successful hedge fund at the exact bottom of the Nasdaq in October 2002. I closed said hedge fund at nearly the exact top in October 2007 when I become an anchor of my own primetime news show on out of the Waldorf-Astoria's famed Bull & Bear Bar which became Fox Business' most popular show for a long time. I signed a deal to become the first ever Wall Street correspondent for The Tonight Show. And I packed up and lately have been successfully investing and trading my own money from my dream ranch back in my hometown in rural New Mexico.

But it's not like it has been all sunshine and profits. Far from it. Let me be clear that during those same years that sound so glamorous when stated as above, I also nearly starved while trying to write a novel that nobody wanted to publish, much less read. I lived with cockroaches and rats in tiny rented apartments near Harlem, in Borough Park, and in the Parade Grounds in Brooklyn. I lost everything on 9/11. I had a more than 50% drawdown and was down 40% at one point on the year while I ran that hedge fund. I vomited almost every morning while I ran other people's money. I was mocked for how small my hedge fund was by Maria Bartiromo on national TV. I got Bell's Palsy -- which onset during a live broadcast of one of my shows caused by Lyme Disease (now cured) while I didn't have health insurance. And I made so many stupid mistakes that I can't even remember them all.

And that's why I wrote this book. I've been around the Wall Street block for a long time, and I've seen firsthand the best of the best and the worst of the worst.

I've made a lot of money for a lot of people, although like anybody else, there have been other times I've lost money. Sometimes even when everything I planned had played out according to plan. I've worked with people who have made billions, and I've also seen people lose billions. I have interviewed hundreds of CEOs, Senators, Congressmen, celebrities. And most importantly, I've also spoken to tens of thousands of everyday people from all walks of life about how they manage their money, and I've helped them get a handle on what they're doing.

For this book, I've drawn upon everything I've learned over the years. I've tried to cover every topic in a way that will be helpful for the average Joe, but I guarantee that every investor and trader, no matter how experienced and successful, will find a lot of gems in here too.

We've presented the information in a Q&A format that I hope makes the content accessible and enjoyable. There's also a glossary of key terms, concepts and phrases and a helpful bibliography of suggested further reading for those of you who want to dig deeper. You can never be too educated when it comes to your money.

A couple things *not* to expect in this book — a magic silver bullet or immediate short-term gains in your portfolio. This book is to help you make big money and protect your capital over the next 10,000 days, not the next 100 days. The key is to get more investments and trades right than wrong over our entire investment/trading career and to maximize our gains in those we get right while minimizing our losses in the trades and investments we get wrong. I've been high-profile trading and investing successfully for a very long time now and while I've got no magic bullet for you, I am quite confident you will become a better investor and trader by reading and following the lessons offered in this book.

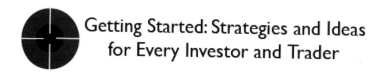

Getting Started: Strategies and Ideas for Every Investor and Trader

Q: What's your overall strategy and approach to investing and trading in the stock market?

A: *In a general sense, my mission is always to find the best companies in the fastest growing sectors and invest in their stocks when they are cheap and to find the worst companies in declining sectors and short them when they are way overvalued.*

Q: How do you come up with many of your ideas that you invest in both on the long or short side?

A: I'll give you two examples of how I come up with my ideas for trades because there are two primary ways I do it.

I shorted the Dollar Stores in 2012 as a "top down" idea, meaning that I looked at the industry from the top down and then I had my team drill down and gather a ton of research and analysis for any Dollar Stores-related play. In this specific example, the idea of shorting the Dollar Stores came to me when I couldn't believe that our rural town here in NM was about to get a bunch more new Dollar Discount Stores even though we already had a bunch here. I've seen the retail sector cycle play out many times and the key to trading/investing in retail is to catch these chains when they are in expansion mode and to sell them when they get to saturation mode.

So my brain started turning because I knew that these Dollar Stores stocks are all up 500-1000% in the last few years as they were in the perfect storm for them to grow — a massive consumer "trade-down" in looking to pay less as the unemployment rate skyrocketed and the average household net worth collapsed 40% just as these guys were getting into the cookie-cutter expansion mode. So my brain started telling me maybe we've got a great storm of our own here to try to catch the top of this classic retail sector cycle. So I sent my guys to work and started doing my analysis and holy cow — the more I worked on the set up, the more excited I got. So by the time I'd spoken to every retail analyst and money manager I know and they all, even the most bearish of them, thought my analysis made tons of sense but that they still thought these Dollar Stores are going to go through the roof from these levels, I started writing for you guys and picking the two best plays to bet against the Dollar Store boom. Now to be clear, I could still be wrong on this trade, but that is what we're here to find out.

Another example I'll give you is called "bottom up" analysis and I used it when buying Apple back in the spring of 2003. After spending years analyzing stocks, I've memorized a lot of company's balance sheets and earnings multiples and things like that. I knew that Apple had a huge pile of cash in the bank, $8 per share to be exact at the time. And I have thousands of stock tickers blinking in front of me and I saw Apple drop 10% or so two or three days in a row as rumors circulated around the tech world that Apple was going to be buying Warner Music Group. I thought that sounded absolutely nuts and so I called around to my Apple sources (which at the time were much more forthcoming with what the company was about to do) and they also thought that sounded absolutely nuts.

So when Apple got to $7 a share — meaning that I was buying the company essentially for free and that any future earnings would simply be gravy...I started buying Apple. As the company rolled out the iPod and its other iOS platforms soon thereafter, I saw the potential for Apple to change the way we were consuming music and I started telling my subscribers that within a couple years Apple would be the world's largest music retailer. At the time, they had less than 5% of the market. They were indeed the world's largest music retailer just a couple years later. And as Steve Jobs started rolling out better and more functional iPods, I started telling everybody that the company would in a couple years start selling "iMiniMacBookPros For Your Pocket" — the iPhone as it turned out. So I stuck with my Apple because my "bottom up" analysis, meaning I found the stock individually based on analysis for it and it alone, and not necessarily for the entire sector. *"Top Down" means you start with a sector or an economic concept and then drill down. "Bottom Up" means you start with an individual company and then move up to analyze its place in that sector and the broader economy.* I use both Top Down and Bottom Up all the time.

Q: How do you get started with your first trade? How much of each stock do I buy when I start building my portfolio?

A: You want to try to have your cake and eat it too — *start off by putting 1/3 as much money as you want to eventually invest into the top 5 or 6 stocks that you have done your homework on* and want to invest in and put some more in after a few weeks in whatever stocks are rated highest at that point and so on. Use scales and don't rush in. Always have plenty of cash and/or income to be able to sleep at night no matter what happens to the markets.

Q: What is your reason behind investing in "only" twelve to fifteen stocks instead of many more, say up to twenty or thirty different stocks? It would de-risk the portfolio a little.

A: Two primary reasons: If you over-diversify, you will limit your gains over time, so I want to be at least somewhat concentrated in my names and have some cash on hand to buy more. Instead of the adage "don't have your eggs in one basket" I prefer "have your eggs in a small number of baskets—and watch those baskets!" I've seen really smart fund managers, time and time again, buy a stock their really smart friend at another fund likes, and they don't focus on managing their own core and best ideas. And it's hard enough to stay up with twelve to fifteen stocks, doing our homework, analyzing the companies and keeping an edge on any more than fifteen can mean distraction and distraction usually means mistakes and mistakes mean losses.

Q: What are your top three rules for every investor and trader?

A: *Investing Rule #1: It's a game of inches.* Remember when Drew Brees passed Dan Marino for the most yards passed in a single NFL season? The day he got the record, he finished with 36 inches more than Dan Marino had. They each threw for more than 5000 yards in a season, which makes 36 inches less than 1/15,000th of a percentage point of their total. But 36 inches was enough for the record books. Even if you do hundreds or even thousands of trades in a given year, every little cent and every little basis point you can fight for adds up. Indeed, that's exactly why high-speed trading is so important to the Goldmans and J.P. Morgans of today — they're trying to skim inches to add up to another record-setting season of trading of their own.

Investing Rule #2) Accurate pricing is crucial. In the same game that Drew Brees broke the record in, his teammate Darren Sproles ran a kickoff back 98 yards before being pushed out of bounds at the 12 yardline, but the officials spotted it at the 14 instead of the 12, so Sproles only got credit for 96 yards on that play. 24 inches of an official's spotting error on one play. Meanwhile, Brees' record stands by 36 inches? I wonder how many times Dan Marino's spots were off back in 1984 and how many Drew Brees' spots were off in 2011. I guarantee there's more than 1/15,000th of a percentage point in plus/minus on that spotting accuracy over a season's 16 games with 40-50 pass plays per game. Make sure you have a good sense of what your assets, including those illiquid assets like real estate, are really worth, because if you're not accurate in gauging their value, you're likely to over or under estimate how safe/wealthy you really are. And if you're investing in a big bank like JPM or Wells Fargo, you better be comfortable with where they are spotting their own balls on the field. Because if I were a bank investor, I'd be throwing a red flag and asking for an instant-replay.

Investing Rule #3) Don't count your chickens before they hatch. I remember when I was a kid I watched some NFL running back set a team-record for rushing yards in a single season as he ran for a three or four yard gain late in a game late in the season. The team stopped play, did a quick acknowledgement and honoring of the breaking of the record and then got back on the field to run the next play. The running back lost five yards on the next play as he was tackled in the backfield and suddenly the record that was just his was no longer his. The team turned the ball over and the game and the season ended and the guy never got the record back. Sort of like all the people who have made fortunes on paper in their stock portfolios only to see the markets take it all back the next year. Don't give your records back to the markets.

Q: How we do avoid the risk of owning stocks during a market crash?

A: Nothing is easy, there's always risk to investing in anything, stocks can crash even when you think they should rally and there's always the possibility for a black swan or a blue swan or a purple goose. You can't be in the stock market expecting that your portfolio won't ever have some declines and *you have to know that you're not likely to be short/ in cash every time the markets crash — and they will and do crash.* That said, I am confident in my economic and markets analysis; I called the bottom in 2002 and the big stock market crash back in 2008 in print and on TV and then the bottom again in early 2009 (and I've made my share of bad calls in between). I have no magic bullet or crystal ball and we all to navigate the market crashes that do come and go. And we have to make sure we've got money to buy if and when the next crash comes rather than having to sell at the bottom.

Q: Should we sell when the economy is clearly horrible?

A: Here's a chart that answers that question:

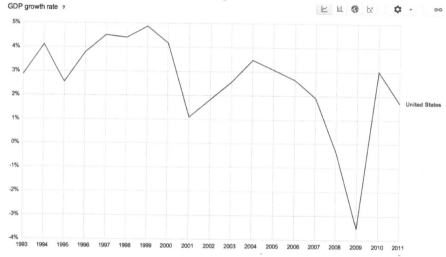

Source: Google Finance and US Federal Reserve

When was the time to sell? Here's a chart of the Nasdaq over the same time frame:

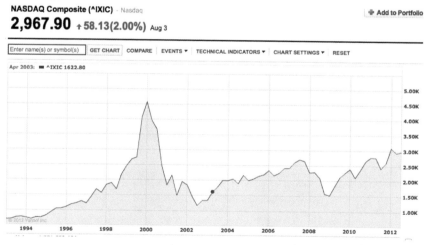

Source: Yahoo! Finance

I make many mistakes, but long-time readers can tell you that two of the greatest calls of my career were when I launched a technology-centric hedge fund in October 2002 with the Nasdaq just twelve days from bottoming after a record 75% drop. And then turned bearish and closed my hedge fund at the top in October 2007 — in large part because of charts like that GDP growth rate one above and other confidence charts hitting those all-time highs and the bubbles around the world looking ripe to pop.

Here's some of what I was writing about at the time in my trading diary at TheStreet.com:

Short Confidence in Long-Side Bets 04:23PM 08/22/07 By **Cody Willard** This isn't the time to be long.

Weekend Vittles: PC to Replace Credit in Your Pocket 03:55PM 07/27/07 By **Cody Willard** By any measure, even with the iPhone numbers, Apple's report this week was impressive.

Caution's Key for This Part of the Cycle 03:52PM 06/12/07 By **Cody Willard** Interest rates and other reasons to get bearish.

Internet Video vs. Cable Companies 03:07PM 06/11/07 By **Cody Willard** Apple's iTunes video rollout is just beginning.

Of Pairs Trades, Pumps and a Deflating Consumer 04:25PM 04/09/07 By **Cody Willard** Matching short ideas with longs will be the order of the next session.

Wait to See the Whites of the Fed Cut's Eyes 02:45PM 03/26/07 By **Cody Willard** The current housing problems are going to cast a wider net and we should listen for the trumpets that sound the sell call.

Avoid Chasing the Pop 09:02AM 03/19/07 By **Cody Willard** Overnight strength in overseas market propels the optimism.

So my question to you again is — when was the time to sell your stocks? You have to "flip it." The time to sell was probably back at the top of that chart when the headlines were screaming about how great the economy was booming back in 2007, not in 2008, for example, when the chart was already in the dumps and so was the stock market.

Sell to the sound of trumpets. Buy to the sound of trumpets. I didn't come up with that advice myself; it comes from one of original Rothschilds.

Will you look at an updated Spain retail sales and confidence chart in three years with the caption "When was the time to buy?"

Think about it.

Q: Why don't we just time the markets and forget about stocks?

A: I do think you can navigate the ups and downs of the short-term by adding to your positions when stocks are down 10-20% and trimming when those stocks are up 20-30% in the short-term. But trading the market swings overall as a strategy is too tough to maintain over the long-term. Every trader and investor, even day traders, have to be concerned about the long-term growth of their portfolios, and over the long run, I trust my analysis and directional bets on both the economy and the stocks I own, so I try to use whatever short-run expectations I've got for the market along with that more fundamental analysis.

Q: Cody, if you anticipate the market to topple, would you go heavily short?

A: *I've seen a lot of brilliant traders and analysts lose their careers over trying to short a crash.* Easy does it. I think most investors should be looking to survive a crash, more than profit from it. And after you survive, pick up good quality businesses for the long term on the cheap from distressed sellers.

Q: Do you use stop losses?

A: I don't use true "stop loss orders" very often as a means of stopping myself out of a position, but I do sometimes draw an informal line in the sand on a position and will sell it out if it crosses that threshold. The fact that I don't use automatic sells very often is in part a reflection of how on top of the markets/trading/investing I am most every day that the markets are open, meaning that I am almost always near enough a broker and aware enough of prices that I can respond intraday. And know the limits of your own discipline. I've been trading for a long time for myself and clients, so my mental line in the sand might be firmer than the average trader's. Retail traders lose the most money when they ignore their own loss thresholds and "just give the stock some time to recover". Sound familiar?

For less active market participants, a GTC (Good to cancel) order can fit the bill for what you're looking for here. Put in an order to sell some of those calls at a price that you would like to lock in part of the profits and if the stock rallies to that price, you'll have it executed automatically.

Q: How do you limit your losses? Do you have a predefined percentage, or it depends on the stock?

A: A decade ago, I was sitting in Jim Cramer's offices down on Wall Street and we were talking about my dream of running my own hedge fund. Cramer had heard from the editor of *TheStreet.com*, where I'd been publishing investment articles for a couple years, that I wanted to launch a fund and he sat down with me several times to give me advice, contacts in the industry and insights into how it all worked. Love Jim or hate him, and if you're in the markets, you probably do one or the other. One thing I have been real smart about throughout my career was to take the good lessons that you learn from anybody you work with and apply them to your own life, your own career, and/or your own approach to the markets.

And one of the best lessons I ever learned from Cramer was to run through your entire portfolio on a regular basis and to rate each stock on a scale from 1 to 10, 1 being "Close this position immediately" and 10 being "Make this position as big as possible as fast as possible." I still do this with the TradingWithCody portfolio every week and it helps guide the weighting of each of the respective positions in my own portfolio, and when a stock's rating falls to 6 or below, I will usually sell it and remove it from the portfolio entirely.

You limit losses by selling/trimming and puking out the longs that aren't working out for you. *Limiting your losses and selling your losers is an art, not a science, but the most important concept is to let your winners work for you and to limit your losses*, including opportunity costs, in those that don't grow to the moon.

Q: Do you have a "percent profit" number in mind where you would sell half of your position and hold the rest?

A: No, there's no set rule for taking profits. If I'd sold even half of my Apple when I made my first 100% on it, I would have missed out on the 1600%. But other times, like with our having caught a huge one day pop in many other shorter-term trades when I have then turned around and sold those calls the next day for a big profit, yes I would sell some of the position and take some profits. It just depends on the analysis, the situation, the timing, etc.

Q: I have a $7k loss in my portfolio for this year. I want to recover these losses in the next two months. What's the best way to do this?

A: You say you have a $7k loss in the portfolio and you want to make it back by year-end. First, if you've only got $7k left in the portfolio, then I would say there's no way you can safely make 100% in the next two months. If you've got $70k left in the portfolio, then you only need to make 10% in the next few months and I would think that's very do-able. As for how best to do it, trying to exactly that is what this whole book is about -- trying to help you find the best way to safely make big money in the markets over time.

Q: Do you use technical or fundamental indicators or talk to your contacts in finding tops and bottoms?

A: F*or my long-term investment theses, I rely on bottom-up fundamental and top-down marketplace analysis.* For short term navigation, I mostly rely on sentiment, psychology and news analysis. I've never drawn a line on a stock chart in my life.

Q: How do you evaluate the management of companies you invest in.

A: Analyzing the managers of a company is a totally qualitative exercise. I don't care what MBA metrics you throw at the problem, it's all about your gut. The best way to train your gut it to listen to lots and lots of earnings calls; you'll start to notice patterns. Listen to the tone of the call and decide if it's overly slick or panicked or smells fishy. Which analysts does management pick to ask questions, the sycophants who want more investment banking business or critical voices? When the CFO talks through the numbers, is she stumbling when explaining a bad result? Is she trying to blame a bad result on really ridiculous external factors? (I've heard CFOs blame everything from mudslides to honeybees for an earnings miss). Does management gloss over the weak areas of their business and do they spend more time telling you what is going right? Does management know less about what's happening at their business than you do and are they spending the call talking about some venture that you know is tanking? (See: Blackberry's Playbook). Do they communicate effectively to Wall Street or are they consumed with playing the quarterly earnings expectations game? Ever notice how Wall Street 's estimates for multi-billion dollar international firms are within a couple hundred thousand dollars? That's not because they're smart, that's because they have access you don't.

Don't invest in companies that are too cozy with the bankers on calls, eventually the hype will fade and those friends will abandon them. *Every CEO has a pretty standard lexicon of fluff phrases that have been endlessly tested by PR people and you need to see through them.* Steer clear of management that is implacable to outside ideas; they are usually more interested in keeping their titles and perks than growing the business.

Stay away from companies where the management and board have big conflicts of interest; they'll be putting their bottom line ahead of your capital. Invest in companies where the management has the courage to do buybacks when the price is battered, not at all-time highs to appease the analysts. Avoid management that pays hugely yielding dividends to keep shareholders around; no company can keep paying out unsustainable amounts of capital for very long. Invest in management teams that you feel have a vision to grow earnings power over time and then keep checking back in to see if they have the ability to change course when something doesn't pan out.

Too much of corporate America is dedicated to extracting huge paychecks, so stay away from management teams that are paid wildly disproportionately to the size of the company or what they have done for shareholders.

Q: What about investing in "take over" plays?

A: There's a lesson that I've learned over the years, best communicated by my old mentor James Cramer back when we used to sit down on a regular basis to go through the positions and strategies in my hedge fund. Almost every time I mention something I learned from Jim Cramer, I get a bunch of angry comments from readers. And let me be clear — Cramer's writings and seemingly often daily flip-flopping on his stock picks and market calls and what not drive me crazy too. And Cramer and I don't talk anymore because he got mad when I went to Fox Business and became a TV guy myself. Anyway, I learned a ton of stuff from Cramer and I'm not shy about using lessons I've learned no matter where I learned them or from whom I learned them. And Cramer taught me that a company being an acquisition target is never enough in its own right to own a stock. It's great to own a stock that is cheap and growing and has other catalysts that is in addition to that, an acquisition target.

Q: What are your thoughts on momentum trading?

A: I think most momentum traders blow themselves and their investors up repeatedly and much more often than is needed as they chase and then flee the momentum. That said, there are some great momentum traders/investors out there and as in most things when it comes to trading/investing, I'd say, "Whatever works, as long as it's legal and ethical." In the grand scheme of the universe, I do not think that the markets and modern-day capitalism will reward "momentum trading" over time and over the long-run. I do use "momentum trading" in some sense myself though, as you'll see me try to lean against the momentum traders when the momentum turns to euphoria and/or buy against them when the momentum subsides and turns to panic.

Q: What are your top three signs of a panic vs. a non-panicked/run-of-the-mill dip?

A: My personal top three signs of a panicky dip are:
1. The headlines are all dominated with gloom and doom and explanations and reasons that you should be panicking.
2. The bears I talk to are gloating and the bulls I talk to aren't just selling, but selling their key holdings into the downturn, and are sick to their stomachs.
3. The sell-off, even at just 5%, is so straight down and so clearly full of panicky selling, that you can't miss it. That doesn't mean it will be easy to buy and that it won't be hard not to follow the panicky bulls and sell, but you'll know the panic is there when it's so hard to buy you can't believe you're pulling the trigger.

Q: Your top 3 signs of a panicked drop did not include a spike in the VIX. Was this a deliberate omission?

A: It was not a deliberate omission per se but the VIX taken in isolation is more random than most analysts admit. Of course, all of my Top 3 Signs of Panic are somewhat objective in their own right, and as always, trading is more of an art than a science. The VIX is often presented as a straightforward measure of volatility, which it's not, so let's define it properly. The VIX is the ticker symbol of a Chicago Board Options Exchange contract, based on an index that measures the implied volatility of options on the S&P 500 index. Which is a fancy way of saying that a bunch of geeks and quants came up with a way to measure how much hedging and options buying market participants are doing at any give time, and relating that to those participants expectations of where the market is headed in the short term. So the VIX is about predicting future volatility, not current volatility, which is why it's called "the fear index". Is your head spinning yet? The part you should pay attention to is the headline quoted number, not how the contract is constructed. A VIX of 40 or above probably means it's time to be buying stocks and a VIX of 10 or below probably means it's time to sell. Lots and lots of other factors go into that decision of course, and only the most experienced market practitioners should ever trade VIX options and futures.

Q: Why do you buy common stock at times and other times you buy calls? What factors go into your decision?

A: There are lots of factors that go down into deciding between common and calls. Some factors include:
1. How expensive are the traders pricing the calls? If the calls let me get long-term upside leverage cheap, meaning that I'm not paying a big premium on the call options, I'll usually put in a little bit of capital there, even if I also own the common.
2. Do I expect near-term catalysts? If I do, then I'll get more aggressive in the calls, even if I have to pay up on the premiums.
3. How much common do I have in the name and how long have I held it? That is a nuanced factor, but one that seems to play into my decision-making on common-vs-calls often.
4. How liquid are the calls I'm considering? You'll want to look at the "open interest." "Open Interest" is just the number of contracts that weren't settled in the last trading session. Generally the bigger the number, the more likely your trade will go through.
5. Does the bid/ask spread on the option look reasonable? If the difference between what the market is bidding for that particular

option from what the market is selling that particular option for is too wide, then you probably want to steer clear. Deciding what is "too wide" is up to debate at best and an utter art form at worst, but if the option is, say 10% or 15% or so, then think twice and make sure you're not overpaying for that option.

Q: When you're trading equities and options, what ratio do you try and stick to?

A: I'd try to keep no more than 1/3 in options relative to each individual longer-term common stock holdings. And overall in the portfolio, I'd be careful to never go over 25-33% or so in options relative to the overall holdings in common stock. *And let me be clear — Don't do any options trading unless you really, really know what you're doing with calls and puts and strikes and expirations.* Unless you feel 100% comfortable with the ins and outs of options and how they work, just stick with common stock.

Q: When you buy a stock for a trade what are you looking for, a couple of points or more? Is there a formula you go by?

A: I'm usually looking to make a double or a triple or even 10x my original investment or more when I invest in a stock. When I trade a stock for a shorter-term trade, I might be looking for 10-30% or so. A wise man once said, "a trade is a trade is a trade," and others have said, "Never let a trade become an investment." The point being that I am flexible in my trading vs. my investing approach but I am always aware of which is which.

Q: When you love a stock you bought higher, but it declines fast along with 20-30% declines in almost every stock on the market, is it a more compelling buy at the lower levels? Do you get scared when your stocks decline?

A: Every time a stock goes down after I buy it, I am scared. Every time a stock goes up after I buy it, I am scared. Every time a stock goes sideways after I buy it, I am scared. I am always scared to expose my capital to potential for capital losses and for the potential of market crashes and the potential for fraud at the companies I've invested in and so on and so forth. Fear comes with investing and is magnified when trading. Stocks and the markets will go up and they will go down and sometimes I'll have huge gains and they'll just seem like they'll keep coming forever and other times I'll have losses and they'll seem like they won't ever stop. *It's all about trusting that your analysis and your ability to get many more trades and investments right than wrong over the next 10,000 or 20,000 days* and knowing that you've done everything you can do to maximize your gains and minimize your potential losses. Even if you're day trading, you obviously are doing so because you want to be in this game making money at the markets for the next 10,000 days, not just tomorrow or the next thirty days. And even if you're day trading, you have to plan for both hot and cold streaks that will come and you have to know and be able to handle that some of those hot and cold streaks will last longer and shock you more than you'd ever thought possible. And that over the next 10,000 days, all investors and traders need to get more trades right than wrong and maximize their gains while minimizing their losses as they do so, no matter their time-horizons for each individual position and no matter what's going on in the economy or the broader markets.

Q: I wanted to ask you if you could recommend a book, a course or maybe a degree that could allow me to understand all technology and the revolutions you invest in.

A: I sometimes teach a college course called "Revolutionomics" and in it I always start my students out with the book *Information Rules* by Hal Varian and Carl Shapiro. It's an excellent tutorial of the major concepts that drive technological markets. That said, I always shock my students when we open class on the fourth week with me throwing a copy of "Information Rules" in the trash all dramatically and then explaining how much of those concepts have been thrown out the window with the advent of the Internet and the ability for users to always find a better/freer/more agnostic alternative. Also, be sure to check out the Bibliography and Suggested Readings at the end.

Q: To what extent does "valuation" play into your stock buying equation?

A: Valuation usually plays a huge part in my investments, but I'll often use different metrics to determine a valuation — for a big cap stock like Apple, I focus on its enterprise value (total market cap - net cash balance) to earnings multiple (or EV/E). In other, small company investments, I might consider the position to simply be a small cap/venture capitalist style investment that will either pay off 10-fold or will be a 50% loss.

Q: What kind of growth do you look for in your long-term stock picks?

A: Secular growth versus cyclical growth is one of the most important concepts for any investor to understand. And *one of the most important elements to successful long-term investing is to making sure we stay long companies positioned for secular growth* and not just cyclical growth.

Secular growth means that demand is going to rise regardless of what the broader economy does. Cyclical growth means that demand will rise and fall along with the cycles of the broader economy.

Revolution Investing means being aware of both the broader economic cycles as well as finding secular stories, such as the burgeoning exploding demand for all things cloud-related and app-related names in here in the early 21st century, for example. Demand for application software, or apps, usage of apps, reading about apps, building of apps, and everything else app-related is going to rise this year over last year and next year over this year and so on and so forth for the next decade or so ... no matter what happens with the broader economic cycle, see?

On the other hand, I'll also try to find shorts in the companies who are losing out because they are on the wrong side of the secular growth phase of such secular changes. Such stocks typically pay off even bigger if the economy were to tank because the business is going to deteriorate regardless of what happens in the broader economy.

Q: How do you know when to close a short position?

A: I consider what my original thesis was and what my short has done. Being short is way different from being long; there's a cap to how much you can make and your losses can technically be unlimited (not possible of course, your brokerage would just liquidate your account if you didn't keep funding your position). Just like being long, it's totally possible to be exactly right about the macro environment, the company you're shorting, and everything else under the sun, and still lose money. The market doesn't work on your schedule. When I'm considering what to do with a short position that is in the green, I check if my thesis has played out and how much more I can make.

If I'm targeting an outright fraud and the company still exists, I'll likely stay short till it gets de-listed or hits penny stock levels. If it's a short position that's a hedge, I constantly solicit opinions that tell me I'm wrong, and I'll close it out if it has done its job hedging a long. If I'm targeting a company that I think is overvalued and the position runs against me, I go back and look at all my original motivations, see if the facts have changed or if I missed something the first time around. *That's why you build positions over time, so you can add to them when the price moves in your favor* (of course it might never do that but over your trading career the discipline of sizing positions relative to your portfolio pays off way more than jumping 100% into any one idea).

And before earnings season, if a company I'm short is being shorted by everyone else (short interest is high) I'll look and see if they expectations have been beaten down so much that the stock could rally with the smallest of good news.

That's what's called a short squeeze, when a lot of traders cover the same short at the same time and they're all forced to buy the stock at once, causing a big spike in price. I also consider whether the company has gotten so cheap that I should actually be long and if there's an acquirer out there circling, looking to pick up the company for a song.

Q: I've often heard my brokers tell me the phrase, "Don't Fight the Fed." Should I listen to them?

A: "Don't fight the Fed." I've been hearing that ol' saw since I first got to Wall Street in 1996. The brokers at Oppenheimer would tell me that when the Fed's raising rates, the markets get hurt. When the Fed's lowering rates, the markets benefit.

Their logic centered around the liquidity and money supply changes that the Fed rate moves affect. In other words, the conventional wisdom says that when the Fed pumps more money into the economy, the stock market will go up and when the Fed drains money from the economy, the stock market will go down. On the surface, the logic makes sense.

But like most things in the market, making sense is often only skin deep and following conventional wisdom is always a bad idea. Turns out that listening to that the conventional wisdom of never fighting the Fed has been the exact wrong thing for a trader to do for the last fifteen years.

Take a look at the chart below that shows the Fed Funds Rates for the last half a century. Focus in on the chart starting in about 1992 or so when you see the Federal Reserve stopped lowering rates:

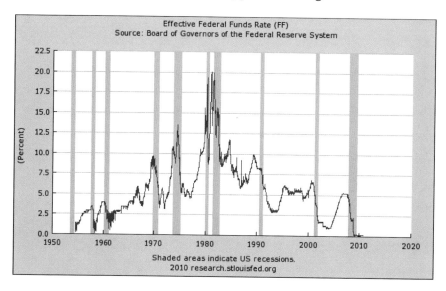

The Fed actually started raising rates in 1994 and if you had stopped at any point from 1992 when the Fed stopped "accommodating" the markets through the year 2000, a full eight years later as the Fed had been moving rates pretty steadily higher, you would have missed out on a 250% rally in the Dow Jones Industrial Average DJIA -0.25% .

Take a look at a chart of the DJIA over just about the same time period as the prior Fed Chart:

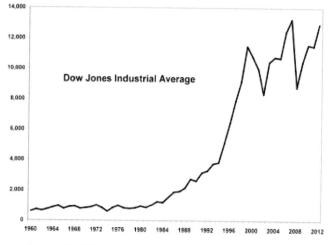

Yes, the boring ol' DJIA was up more than triple in the eight years that the Fed was mostly raising rates. People who thought they shouldn't "fight the Fed" were left sitting on the sidelines.

And then if those same people followed that same logic and started buying stocks as the Fed started (drastically) lowering rates in late 2000 and into early 2003, they would have seen their investments get outright crushed. I mean, the DJIA was down nearly 40% in that time frame (the Nasdaq Composite was down 75% while the Fed was cutting rates!).

In 2003, the Fed started raising rates again, and what did those folks who thought they should get out of the market because they didn't want to fight the Fed see the markets do while they sat on the sidelines after taking their huge losses by "not fighting the Fed" in the couple years prior? They missed an 80% move in the DJIA as the markets nearly doubled as Fed steadily moved interest rates higher.

Finally, in 2007 and 2008 as the Fed moved rates down to 0%, taking them as low as they can go, what did those folks get for "not fighting the Fed?" The market dropped about 60%.

Q: How do I trade to minimize my taxes?

A: You don't. It's hard enough to invest successfully without trying to minimize what Uncle Sam's going to take at the end of the year. *If your catalyst for selling a position is based on tax strategy instead of maximizing your gains and minimizing losses, you're bound to hamper your own long-term performance.* You have to be focused on making money and not saving money if you want to make money. For other Investing and Trading No-no's, please see Chapter 4.

Q: Can you share with us what your general investment portfolio looks like as of the summer of 2012?

A: Real Estate- I've been buying land in NM and I've just moved into a house that I designed and built and have thus far paid for with cash out of pocket so that I don't have a mortgage so that I don't take on the risk of securitization/mis-payment/etc. that comes with a bank mortgage. I've done some owner-financing of the land when the terms have been attractive (some of the land I've bought has been at 70% off where it was listed at the top less than a handful of years ago for example). For years on my TV show and on my blogs, I told people that I thought real estate was a terrible investment. That is no longer the case. I think real estate is a great investment in many places right here. Right here, right now, I'd guess that real estate is not quite half of my portfolio, but again — my portfolio is changing every day, every month and every year, so any estimate can be misleading.

Content generation- I've been steadily growing my content generation businesses for more than 12 years now, since I first built Teleconomics.com, my first subscription-based website that many of you here still recall. I've grown the content generation source of income to the point where it can support me if I need it to and it continues to grow from years past, including from the time I'd been a TV anchor for 528 shows over 2.5 years at Fox Business. I am not sure I'd ever go back to managing other people's money or doing a TV show for a living again since I love doing what I do right now. I especially enjoy what I am doing TradingWithCody.com.

Stock market- I have made some great money in the last few quarters in the stock market since I returned to the stock market. But I do not ever count on the market for steady gains or for income. EVER.

Bonds- None. I'll probably get short Treasuries and corporate bonds and other bonds when/if
the debt/bond/Treasury bubbles finally burst.

Oil, gold and other commodities - I'm generally looking to build up short positions in gold, silver and in oil, but at the current time, I have very little exposure to oil, gold or other commodities. We're likely to see inflation in the things we need, such as food and clothes, and deflation in the things we own, such as gold and oil.

Actual Business (e.g. selling products, or providing a service)- The books and TradingWithCody.com and building WallStreetAllStars.com are a big part of my income and they continue to grow.

Q: Are you building multiple streams of income?

A: Yes, I try to make sure I diversify my income streams. I think *diversifying one's income streams is much more important in the long run than trying to diversify one's assets.*

Options Demystified:
Calls, Puts and Leaps, Oh My!

Q: What's the best way to get started trading options?

A: *You should not trade options at all until you've been reading me and other sources on how to trade options.* I'd suggest creating a fake brokerage account where you can trade options on paper so that you can learn more.

Q: What do you think of doing more sophisticated options trading, such as unwinds, spreads, straddles, etc.?

A: I don't typically do unwinds and spreads, etc., with my options trades. I do a lot of homework and expect that my directional bets will work out okay over time.

Q: Do you ever sell put options when you expect a stock to rally or short a call options when you expect a stock to drop?

A: I rarely short options. What's the point? You can lose infinite if the trade goes against you and you can only make up to 100% if the trade works out. That said, there are times when I do think it makes sense because the set up is steady-betty action but you don't think there could be much upside from the levels you're looking at.

Q: Should I sell my options, for example, my calls, whenever I have a big gain on them?

A: Not necessarily. Here are two ways you can trade those calls now so you can have your cake and eat it too:

1. The less sophisticated investor and/or those trading with small portfolios, of say, less than $100,000 or so (in which commissions of the more aggressive trading I detail below eat too much into capital) should just sell half the calls they bought back then. Take the cash from those proceeds and just leave it be for now.

Keep the rest of the calls and let them ride for now. If the stock rallies up a bunch more before those calls expire, you can sell another half of what's left and likely have almost tripled your money at that point on this trade. Let whatever remaining calls you have left ride into their expiration and then just keep the shares. If the stock drops back below your strike and, heaven forbid, doesn't come back in time for the expiration, you've still locked in some big gains and have no losses on the trade.

2. Back when I was running a hedge fund for a living and I was executing dozens of trades per day most days. I'd always look to create "positive gamma" in my positions like this. Positive gamma is just a fancy way of saying that you're positioning yourself to profit more than you can lose, no matter what the stock does.

Let's say you bought 100 of the March $500 calls on Google back a while ago for $20 or so. Say the stock has spiked and those calls are now trading at $48 per contract. But instead of selling half, you go out and short 5000 shares of Google. Since 100 calls gives you the rights to 10,000 shares of Google, you've just locked in half the profit.

Let's say the stock falls to $300 a share now. Well, guess what — you're short 5000 shares for a $200 drop from the current $520 levels. That would be $100,000 in profits. Of course, you'd lose your entire investment in the calls, but since you paid $20,000 for those calls, you still profit big time from the trade. Meanwhile, if the stock continues to climb and gets to, say $600 a share, those calls will have kept going up in value — at a faster pace than the stock itself, of course, to account for the time value in the options — and you'd be sitting on a $40,000 loss from the shorted shares (5000 at $80 loss, as the stock ran from $520 to $600 after you shorted half as many shares as your call options represent).

The calls would be worth about $110 or $120 or so depending on how volatile the stock and the markets have been at that point, and you'd have $110,000 to $120,000 profit in those calls.
Positive gamma. It's a great position to strive to put yourself into, but you do have to:

a) know exactly what I mean by all of the above and understand thoroughly the math and the numbers in the math that I laid out above.

b) and be trading with enough capital so that the slippage and commission costs that come with aggressive trading don't eat your nest egg away.

Q: What do you think of just shorting market puts as an overall strategy, which can be a killer in a crash, but the time premium works for you in a flat or rising market.

A: From Victor Neiderhoffer to James Altucher, I've learned from many great traders the ups and downs of shorting puts. It works great when it works, but I've seen Victor wipe out years worth of gains by shorting puts when a bull market turned bear.

Q: What do you think about buying warrants as a sort of equivalent for call options?

A: Warrants don't usually trade as liquidly as options which don't exactly trade liquidly anyway. If you're making long-term bets and can get a fair price on warrants, then thumbs up, but I wouldn't use them as a short-term trading vehicle.

Q: Do you recommend LEAPS on some of your favorites or do you prefer common?

A: I like calls, call LEAPS (LEAPS are options that expire say, 12 months out or more) or common, but using any calls will be wildly volatile and risky along the way. LEAPS on this high of a beta stock are expensive, which adds to their risk, but options give you a way of capturing leverage with a little amount of capital as the stock moves. You have to decide on your own what's reasonable for you.

Q: If you want to buy calls that expire in say, six months, does it make a difference if you buy calls that are closer to the asking price but more expensive or further away from asking price but less expensive?

A: Yes, it does matter and here's how. *You get more upside leverage when you buy the cheaper calls with the higher strike prices, but there's a lot more risk* because the stock would need to rally higher to get past those strikes so that you are in the money. And the longer out the expiration dates, the more "time slippage" you have as you are paying a premium for having a longer time before the options expire, which is obviously valuable because stocks can make a huge move in the extra month or six months or whatever time you're paying up for. Buying a long-dated call with a higher strike price is risky and expensive, so you don't want to risk more money than you can afford to lose of course. On the other hand, if the stock blows past your strike price and you were able to buy a bunch more call options than you would have if you'd bought lower strikes, you'd have much more profits than if you'd just bought fewer of the lower priced call options. Risk and reward are reflected in the costs. So be careful no matter what you do whenever you use any options.

Q: If you have calls that are well in the money, how long can you hold them before time decay has an impact?

A: With options that are well into the money, there's not much time decay to worry about. Time decay really hurts holders of out-of-the-money options because you're literally paying for a time premium since the option is technically not worth anything but a bet that eventually the underlying contract will be of value. "Eventually" being the operative word in that last sentence. On the other hand, when you're far-in-the-money already on your options, most of the premium is charged because it allows owners of the options to control much more stock for less capital, so long as the options remain in the money. So the answer to your original question is that you don't really need to worry too much about time decay on those options while they're far in the money. Of course, you have risk and a lot of it in those far in-the-money options too. Because if the stock falls down to where your strike price is, the value of those options fades much more on a percentage basis than the underlying common stock and if the stock doesn't come back above those strikes before they expire, you can lose the entire capital you had invested in them even as Apple continues on its way to $1000 over the next few years. Take some profits, keep some exposure, buy some higher-priced and longer-dated calls than you currently own when the stock is down next time. That's how I'd do it.

Q: How do you determine if the "premium" you're paying for an option is "cheap" or "expensive?"

A: I'll give you a real-world example of "cheap premium" vs. "expensive premium" from my service TradingWithCody.com where I post all my trades in real-time:

I just bought some more Visteon common. I thought the call options on this one, which has been trading in a $20 range between $60 and $75 for the last year, would be cheaper than they are right now. This stock's kind of range performance for such a sustained period of time would normally translate into the call options having some cheap-o premiums. But in this Visteon case right now, let's break it down for you why I think the calls are too expensive.

If I were to buy the December 2011 call options for Visteon, here are the prices I'd have to pay right now:

     Dec 11 VC calls with a $55 strike go for $11.90
     Dec 11 VC calls with a $65 strike go for $6.50
     Dec 11 VC calls with a $70 strike go for $5

Visteon sells for $62 a share right now, meaning you can buy 100 shares for $6200. Alternatively, looking at the prices I give you for the December 2011 call options with various strike prices, you can see that you get more leverage for less money. Specifically, in the Visteon example above, those prices I list mean that if you were to buy the right to sell someone 100 shares of Visteon stock on the third Friday of December at $55 per share (which are currently "in-the-money" because the stock is above that price), it would cost you $1190. The right to sell it at the higher price of $70 would cost you only $500 because $70 is "out-of-the-money" while the stock is below that price (and the current quote of the stock at $62 per share is obviously below $70, right?). Of course, as I often remind you dear subscribers, when we buy options, we can lose 100% of the capital risked if the stock isn't on the right side of the strike before the expiration date.

Meanwhile, given that Broadcom is currently at just under $22 per share, fully double where it was this time last year when I first started highlighting it as "the next Apple" for readers, you would think that the options in that name would be more expensive given such a big move higher. Here are the current quotes for the same expiration date as Visteon's call options above, the December 2011 near-the-money call options, for Broadcom:

Dec 11 Broadcom calls with a $20 strike for $3.50
Dec 11 Broadcom calls with a $22 strike go for $2.45
Dec 11 Broadcom calls with a $24 strike go for $1.70

With Broadcom currently at about $22 a share that means you can buy 100 shares for Broadcom for $2200. And yes, looking at the prices I give you for the December 2011 call options with various strike prices, you can see that you get more leverage for less money. Specifically, in this Broadcom example, those prices I list mean that if you were to buy the right to sell someone 100 shares of Broadcom stock on the third Friday of December at $20 per share, it would cost you $350. The right to sell it at the higher price of $24 would cost you only $170 because $24 is "out-of-the-money" while the stock is below that price (and the current quote of the stock at $22 per share is obviously below $24, right?).

So which options, if either give you the better bang for your buck?

With the in-the-money call options I outline there above, you can buy the right to control 100 shares of Visteon stock at 10% below the current quote (the $55 strikes) for $1190 or about 19% of what it would cost you to just buy 100 shares of the common stock, which would cost you $6200. Meanwhile, you can buy the right to control 100 shares of Broadcom stock at 10% below the current quote (the $20 strikes) for $350 or about 16% of what it would cost you to buy 100 shares of Broadcom common stock, which would cost you $2200.

With the out-of-the-money call options I also outline above, you can buy the right to control 100 shares of Visteon stock at 10% above the current quote (the $70 strikes) for $500 or about more than 8% of what it would cost you to just buy 100 shares of the common stock, which would cost you $6200. Meanwhile, you can buy the right to control 100 shares of Broadcom stock at 10% above the current quote (the $24 strikes) for $170 or closer to 7% of what it would cost you to buy 100 shares of Broadcom common stock, which would cost you $2200.

In other words, it costs more premium to buy the rights to sell people Visteon stock at both in-the-money and out-of-the-money strike prices than it does for to buy the rights to sell people Broadcom stock with the same variables. Yet, Broadcom is a much more volatile stock and has been performing tremendously on both the fundamentals and on the stock price in the last few quarters. *Take the pitches that the markets give ya'.*

Q: Is it always best to place an option trade closer to the Friday in the third week of the month to get the most available time for the trade to develop?

A: The 3rd Friday of the month is simply an arbitrary recurring date that Wall Street has long used as the option expiration date for most options you'll buy. I mostly buy options that give me 3-12 months of time before they expire and only rarely will you guys see me do a short-term option trade and only then because I think I see a clear near-term catalyst.

Trading, Surviving and Profiting on Earnings Reports

Q: I've noticed that you like earnings plays when you have a contrarian opinion. What sources do you use as your yardstick against your view?

A: The main sources I use as my yardstick are analyst reports. I read dozens of tech analyst reports every morning — from analysts at JPM, Gleacher, Goldman, etc. They don't give you much information other than what the consensus and group-think is looking for. And that information is invaluable when it comes to trying to game an earnings report. I've been reading these reports every day and doing these types of trades for 15 years now and you can see the patterns. Though sometimes I'll still be wrong.

Three things I do before ever considering putting on a trade into an earnings report: I gauge how the quarter went relative to consensus estimates; gauge the sentiment around the stock; and gauge how other stocks have been trading after they report earnings.

Q: Where we can follow analysts at JPM, Gleacher, Goldman, etc?

A: I get those reports because I ran a hedge fund and traded with those guys and then became a D-list Wall Street celebrity TV star and they keep sending me the reports for free without my ever asking them too. Stock market research is still not a level-playing field for the average guy at home.

Q: What's the best way to hedge your long positions going into earnings?

A: You will see some outsized gains if your long positions report strongly and the stocks rally after the reports. You'll cut into those potential gains if you spend money on "hedging" those positions. But then again, as one of my old mentors, a successful hedge fund manager named Jay Burnham, used to say "May you lose money on all your hedges" because that usually means you're making big money on your actual investments/bets. Anyway, if you're worried that you're too heavily long both common and calls heading into the earnings reports and you want to hedge, I would suggest a pure hedge of buying some near-term slightly-out-of-the-money puts. I'd probably look at buying about enough of the puts to cover at least the common stock portion of your longs and then your calls still let you catch the upside of any major near-term rally in the underlying stock (and they'll even open you up to some positive gamma but let's not get distracted with Greek terms here). You could also look at shorting some calls with different times and strikes than the ones you currently are long to create different hedging strategies within each position, but I tend to think that most traders who do that stuff end up spending more time and energy and commissions and slippage than makes it worth it. From time to time I have bought or shorted an ETF to capture a macro theme, but I don't like to do this in general. Finally, you could find a stock that you think you could "pair" with each of your stocks, meaning that you short a similar stock to, say, F (in F's case you could consider GM a potential "paired" hedge), and hope that the rally in the stock you are long far outpaces the rally in the stock you are short as its pair.

Q: What would a good strategy be for collaring so you can get an upside potential and a downside potential no matter how a stock reacts to its earnings report? Whether it spikes or crashes, you'd make money, right?

A: The reason I bet on earnings reports the way I do — small and in one direction, rather than any other way, is because it works for me and it has for a long time. When I used to run a hedge fund and I'd do pre-earnings gambles sometimes and would write about it, Jim "Rev Shark" De Porre asked me a very similar question and used to pester me when I'd get a pre-earnings directional trade wrong. So I went back and tracked every single pre-earnings directional trade I'd done since I'd launched the fund and found two things: One, I got about 65-70% of the directional bets right. Two, when I got those directional bets right, I made 2-3x my money because I'd stuck with betting on just one direction and not hedging it and thereby guaranteeing a lower return on the capital outlayed into the trade. I would venture to guess that my track record on these pre-earnings trades since I launched TradingWithCody.com are indeed still running at about 65-70%. Read "Bringing Down the House" the book by Ben Mezrich about six MIT students who took Vegas for millions playing Black Jack, for more on the concept of statistically significant tracking while maximizing returns.

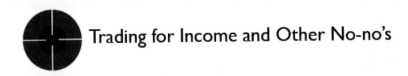 Trading for Income and Other No-no's

Q: I am going to retire soon and will need to do some short term trades to make up my income, any suggestions who to follow for short term trades?

A: Oh no! *I'm not joking when I tell people that I think trading for income is always a bad idea.* I think it's a truly awful idea for somebody who's leaving the labor force to retire. Trading profitably is hard enough over time. But trading profitably and trying to live off that income is going to prove to be as impossible for you as it has been for everybody I've ever seen try it. Think of it this way – you know that even the world's best trader is going to get cold sometimes. I've seen guys who made 1000% per year for five years lose 30% in six months. And then lose another 30% over the next six months because their system/method/analysis/thought-process/whatever missed a nuanced change in the markets. Those guys got wiped out, despite all those years of gains, because they were dependent upon income from that same trading that just went cold to the tune of a 60% loss. How will you know when it's time to take money out of the portfolio? *And if you have a few weeks or months of not making money – and worse – losing money, will you be okay?* Will you want to add more money to the portfolio or take bigger risks to get the money you need back out? It is impossible to consistently, month after month, make enough profitable and few enough losing trades to ensure you have income from trading. I don't mean to stress you out, but I am adamant that trading for income will eventually put you out of the game. I don't advocate trying to trade as a short-term way to make money for your daily needs or to just make enough for a down payment or the next semester of college. Making enough for the big purchases in life is great but only if it's a long-term goal. Trading under the gun is a sure way to double down on misery.

Q: I am trying to work my way back to some trading income after my devastating experience with some unscrupulous stock brokers.

A: I tell everybody that it's a bad idea to try to trade for income. Everybody will have a big "draw down" at some point, which means that you'll fall maybe 20, maybe 30% or more from your all-time highs in your stock account. And when that happens, that means you're going to have to make 40 or 50% or more just to get back to where you were at the highs. Does that mean, if you were trading for income, that you went without any cash flow/income for those months that it took you to get back to your highs? Or does that mean you now keep taking money out even though you're down and you're playing with a fraction of the capital you were at the highs?

Before you make a single trade for income, you should consider what it means to be wrong, consistently, for three months. Or more. No trader I've ever known, and I know some real trading legends, has a spotless record. And human nature being what it is, you'll get desperate when you see all red and it will impact your performance. Why put yourself under that much pressure? There are traders out there who trade for income and do okay and even some who have become pretty wealthy but the average Joe has as much chance of trading for income successfully for the long-term as they do of winning the lottery.

I do think we can continue to consistently blow away the broader markets and make a decent percentage on our capital base when we look at our portfolio over quarters and years. But there will always be months that will be tough when you're cold as ice on your bets and if you're having to force trades at those times because you need income, you're probably going to end up losing even more.

Be careful is what I'm saying. And please consider not trading for income or risking money in options if you don't think you have enough to invest in a one share of a company's common stock.

Q: I have made all the typical trading and investing mistakes. Now, everything is under water and every day it just gets worse. This is where the inexperienced would sell at the bottom. Even knowing that, I can hardly take the pain any longer. I have a cabinet of 200 trading books, seminars, etc. telling me what I should have and could have done. How do I handle this depression?

A: First off, I'm sorry to hear about your pain and I know how bad it hurts. It will get better. Second, unless those books point out the hard truth that I will -- that *every trader and every investor will at some point have a huge draw down from the highs in the portfolios* -- then they are probably mostly worthless. Nothing but perseverance will serve you now. I don't know what's right about buying or selling your particular positions right now, but you're probably right that since holding on is the hardest trade to make right now, it's probably the right one. Stay in the game and good luck.

Q: How do you feel about trading and investing in penny stocks?
A: In general, the rule to investing and trading penny stocks (any stock trading at less than $5 is typically consider a "penny stock") is: *Don't invest or trade penny stocks.*

Because they usually have such small market caps and so few shares outstanding in the markets, they are easily moved higher for the short-term, often enabling insiders and their cronies to run up the stocks temporarily so that they can sell as many shares as they can while the stock is up. Let's talk more about this as there's always a ton of questions from everybody I know about such and such penny stock, and there's some easy flags to see when you should run from a particular penny stock.

A couple years ago, I'd been invited by a friend to a ZZ Top concert at Beacon Theatre in NYC. My friend was friends with Billy Gibbons and Gibbons' wife, who was into the markets and they'd invited me backstage to hang out after the show. We eventually ended up on ZZ Top's tour bus and in between my getting to pick a little bit on Billy's 1960s Les Paul and talking about how much he loves the Inn of the Mountain Gods in Mescalero, NM, his wife and I were talking stocks. And then the conversation turned to a penny stock that she owned and I set the guitar down because I was pretty sure where this talk was about to go.

The stock she wanted to know about was WTER.OB. A ".OB" stock which means that it was either so small or had a rough enough history that it couldn't even get listed on a major exchange. Not all .OB stocks are trash, but most of them are, and that's a huge red flag already. This was before we had iPhones and I wasn't going to sit there and pull up the stock and research it for her on ZZ Top's tour bus anyway, so I told her I'd email her some analysis.

A few months ago, I was at my dad's farmhouse in Hondo Valley when a telephone company utility truck pulled down the drive. Our longtime neighbor hopped out and wanted to know if I had a minute to talk stocks. He wanted to know if I had any opinion about a particular penny stock, RAYS, that he had been told was ready to hop 10-fold. We were out on the farm so I told him I'd take a look at it when I got back to the office and would shoot him an email. But again, hearing a casual investor/trader ask me about a penny stock was already a red flag for me.

Though the details of each of the above anecdotes are worlds apart —
a rock star's wife in NYC and a utility worker in rural NM; WTER made
water purification systems and RAYS does Internet streaming video
compression — it was very easy for me to quickly determine that these
were both screaming "sells" and that I wouldn't touch either stock with
a ten foot pole.

Both stocks collapsed after I warned my friends about them and in fact,
there is no such stock trading under the WTER symbol at all any more.

Take a look at the "news" releases for RAYS at the time my neighbor
was asking me about it and you'll see plenty of red flags right here:

> BUYINS.NET Issues Raystream SqueezeTrigger Report
> *GlobeNewswire (Tue, Dec 6)*
>
> Rapid Growth in Online Video Plays Into Akamai and Raystream's
> Strong Suits *Marketwire (Fri, Nov 25)*
>
> Market Considerations in Europe Outlook – Featured Research on
> Raystream Inc. and Lithium Exploration Group Inc. *Marketwire
> (Thu, Nov 10)*
>
> Breakthrough Technology From Level 3 and Raystream Simplifies
> Online Video *Marketwire (Mon, Nov 7)*
>
> A Turn in Tide, Europe's New Deal – Research Report on
> RAYSTREAM INC and Netflix, Inc. *Marketwire (Fri, Nov 4)*

Marketwire? That's not Marketwatch, people. It's a news wire upon
which anybody or anyone or any company can buy a press release and
Yahoo! Finance and many the other news services will pick it up there
as news. "But," my neighbor asked, "aren't all those research reports
talking about RAYS and NFLX and AKAM saying that this stock and their
technology are about to explode?"

Sure, if those reports are from a reputable research shop, especially if
you are sure that the report writers and the company are wholly arms-
length. But are they? Have you ever heard of the companies issuing that
research? And more to the point, as I mentioned above, are you sure
that the company or its controlling shareholder didn't pay someone to
write that research?

When you see press releases touting a research report touting a penny
stock, I would run for the hills. I haven't played the lottery once in my
life, haven't even contributed a dollar to the office funds when the
jackpot is through the roof, but I would probably rather buy a lottery
ticket than just about any small-cap (less than $250 million market
cap) penny stock.

It's hard enough making money in the market when your research
resources aren't biased. And few small-cap penny stock news releases
and the research reports they tout are unbiased. My old pal Tim Sykes is
making a career out of finding and shorting these kinds of promotional

small-cap penny stocks. That's probably the only way to make any money in penny stocks — shorting them when they're in the spiked promotional phase.

Be careful with your money. I have made a lot of money for a lot of people by buying revolutionary technology companies of any market cap size and shorting companies whose government-sponsored business models are failing. I don't know anybody who's made big money consistently ever in penny stocks. Don't even try.

Q: How do I make up lost ground when I have been greedy and my stocks are not behaving as I had anticipated?

A: Let's break your question down and really get some helpful analysis for everybody out of it. First, it's good that you admit that greed has hurt your performance. Second, it's good to recognize the specific trades that have hurt your performance. *Have you analyzed your losing positions from a fresh perspective? Did you close the losing trades completely and move on? If so, did you remove those stocks from your computer monitors entirely so you don't look at it and fuel your emotions/greed?* Third, and most importantly, you do realize this is still a "greedy" mentality (not that I'm judging, because Lord knows I've certainly been desperate to make up losses before too, just as everybody who has ever traded for any decent amount of time have been): "I have some ground to make up."

You can't force the making up of that ground. You'll end up over-reaching and making desperate trades because you're feeling the pressure of making up that ground. Forget that ground you've lost. It's gone. It's over. Your portfolio is right now what it is. Let's start afresh and figure out how to slowly but surely and safely build up your portfolio to new highs over the next year, two years and five years. Trying to make up that ground by aggressively trading earnings reports this quarter is simply gambling. Fourth, as always, I want to try to remind you not to force any trades. Over time, unforced errors caused from trying to get that ground back will start erasing your gains.

Q: How about buying stocks when they announce they are going to split their stock?

A: So what if the company doubles the numbers of shares outstanding and halves the stock price? *What good does a stock split do for anybody except the bankers, accountants and lawyers who get paid fat fees for pretending to do the hard math involved and making sure the right papers get filed at the right agencies?*

Stock splits might have made some sense back in the early 1900s when the value of a dollar was 90% less than it is today, which would have made a $200 stock equivalent to several-thousand-dollar stock. And back then a higher share count might actually have impacted the ability to trade a stock.

But why on God's green Earth should a company with a $200 or a $500 per share stock price split it? Does the market and its billions of shares traded every day seem illiquid to you? NO! Does a $200-per-share price keep small investors out? NO! (Surely nobody is going to argue that someone who can't afford to put $200 into one share should be investing in stocks.) A stock split for a company and stock like Apple is meaningless and just a distraction.

Q: Do you have a basic 'smell test' for if an investment opportunity is a scam?

A: There are new twists on new scams every day and even the smartest people get tricked. The best way to protect yourself is to recognize a basic framework of how these things go down, because there's nothing new under the sun. When it comes to your money, assume everyone is trying to make you part with it and that what they are telling you is the part they want you to hear. Always ask "How can this go really wrong?". A few years ago I stormed out, telling the audience I wouldn't be any part of an investment panel at a conference I was on when Lenny Dykstra started his presentation by saying "You can't lose with my system". He's now in prison. *If they don't have an exhaustive answer for what can go wrong or if they say it's risk-free, run as fast as you can.*

Q: I received an offer in the mail from a company offering to buy the death benefit to my life insurance policy. I'm considering doing it out so I can have the cash on hand now and invest it in the market. Do you have any advice for me?

A: *Any time you get a lump sum now in exchange for future cash flows or assets you need to be really extra careful.*

There's been a rash of bankruptcies and fraud from companies that make big promises about getting you money upfront for something you only expected to get in the future. I'm not going to name any names and give them free advertising but I'm talking about the structured settlement industry, selling your life insurance policy and reverse mortgages.

There are potential legitimate functions for each of these but it sure is a seedy group of people in these industries. Structured settlements are what you get paid for a lawsuit or worker's compensation or some kind of legal agreement where you get cash over time. The singing mid-day TV commercials that promise you cash today work on the fact that to get a loan against your cash flows you'd probably have to petition a court or change the settlement term or go through spools of red tape. So they helpfully come in, make you feel like they're on your side, and say they'll cut a check right away for your settlement or insurance policy or home.

What they fail to mention, and what they don't make clear when you're on the phone, is that cash will be 20-40% below fair value, they'll bundle your future payments with all their other customers, and sell them as bonds through Wall Street bankers (who got the bonds a Triple-A rating) . And once you dial that 1-800 number the high-pressure tactics start, they'll start telling you all the things you could do with that money "Right now!" (College! A boat! A boat at college!).

Unless you have an absolute urgent, non-negotiable need for that cash up front, don't ever do these deals. They are designed to get more meat for the Wall Street fixed-income sausage factory, not to pay you the real value of the future cash flows. *To any senior considering a reverse mortgage, those pitches are often coupled with an offer of how to invest your cash. Same rules apply, their game is underpayment at the best and at the worst outright fraud.*

Q: I got a call from a number I didn't recognize and it turned out to be a broker who said he was at my old brokerage and was following up because he remembered I like pharmaceutical companies. I've never heard of his new firm but the company he was talking about has a new drug with a double-blind trial and is close to FDA approval. The stock seems cheap especially considering the potential, do you have any advice about how to research the name?

A: You've been targeted by a boiler room. Never pick up a call from that number ever again! Early in my career, when I first arrived in New York from Ruidoso, New Mexico, with zero old-boy network contacts or rich uncles, cracking into the Wall Street hierarchy seemed near impossible.

I eventually landed at Oppenheimer & Co with one of the biggest brokers on the Street, but before that I was offered jobs that I never even considered taking by the scummiest parts of the industry that existed to make a quick buck off the sucker born that day. In a swamp of scum, floating on the surface of the pond scum, were pockets of scummy amoebas known as the boiler rooms. The basic boiler room setup is an anonymous office, brokers working the phones for commission with reams of phone numbers of targets to cold call.

These boiler room shops have names that evoke private banks or reputable trading houses; they all sound vaguely familiar but just a little bit off. The smarter ones buy "212" phone numbers, throw up a website with some generic copy talking about trust and reputation and excellence and rent a tiny room in Manhattan, anything for the appearance of legitimacy.

I'm giving you an unqualified signal to run, hang up the phone, never ever open an account with these people, don't even stay on the phone to humor yourself. The best guys will keep you talking and then slip in something that seems really low-stakes and before you know it you're buying options on Panamian teak carbon credits (believe it or not, that's a real one).

The big scam these guys pull is the "pump-and-dump;" they cold-call enough people to buy a stock they own lots of, that nudges up the price, and then they cash out.

A common tactic is telling you about their "exclusive research" they only share with "institutional investors and the best clients" in the hopes you'll buy the stock they're pushing. And the product they push has changed over time, so don't just be wary of traditional equities.

Since discount brokerages have made talking to a live broker a foreign and expensive concept, the boiler rooms push penny stocks ("It's high-growth, Wall Street doesn't know about it yet, but they'll be on an exchange next year") private placements, private equity deals, private investment in public equity (PIPES), FOREX trades and complex commodities trades that are fee laden. And if you get a voicemail but the caller makes it seem as though they dialed you by accident while trying to call someone else with insider info, congratulations, you've just been targeted by the newest boiler room tactic.

Rule of thumb, if you get a call or email out of nowhere, your number or address was purchased along with thousands of others, and the broker on the other side is playing the numbers game, hoping to get one big fish out a hundred. This is time you want be part of the 99%, and hang up.

Q: There's a mining company that I see in all the trade magazines and advertising its new technology on TV. I want to buy a little just to track the name, everything sounds good and it's in a growth industry, can you tell me how big of a position I should start off on?

A: This is the rare time I can give you really specific advice about your portfolio and the trade: buy exactly $0 of that company's stock. Between those breaks on the financial news networks, you'll often see a corporate ad touting how they are changing the world and at the end they'll flash a ticker symbol alongside their company logo. *Never invest in a stock that you ever see advertised.* Most of these are micro caps or even penny stocks and they're bumping up against securities laws by pushing their ticker. Do you think you'll ever see Coca-Cola or Microsoft advertise their stock? And I'm going to include stocks you see advertised in print and at investment conferences.

Not too long ago I went to a commodities investment conference in midtown Manhattan to see a friend give the keynote address. While walking around the conference floor and saw about 250 companies listed on the Toronto Venture Exchange that had set up "investor relations" booths. The event was being catered with rare Kenyan coffee and Ladurée macaroons imported from Paris. And those investor relations booths were staffed by comely young women who would talk to you endlessly about a new mine in Zambia and the hundreds of millions in revenue that would certainly materialize.

Now if these companies are resorting to pastries and other enticements you'd think people would see this as transparent advertising and run away right? Nope, I had plenty of friends (including that keynote speaker) who had bought shares of companies at the conference.

Stay away from any stock that is advertised ever, including those ETFs and MLPs on TV. Those vehicles especially need lots of investors to make them liquid or they wither and die. You have enough data out there to sort through; just go ahead and disregard any stock that has to advertise for your attention.

Q: My accountant introduced me to an investment adviser who is telling us to take advantage of a change to the tax code and buy a product from a life insurance company through a trust. The logic seems to check out and the investment adviser has done this for lots of other investors. What do you think?

A: The whole deal is laden with conflicts of interest and I'd tread very carefully. Here's the basic precept I want burned into your mind: *no money ever changes hands without an angle and you have to know the angle of the person on the other side before you let even a dollar out of your grasp.* Seriously, no one is your friend or wants to make you rich or is letting you in on a special deal because they like you.

Investing because someone has a magnetic personality or because they work for a big investment bank is the surest way to lose money. Beware geeks bearing formulas and beware bankers bearing financial products. It isn't just the small investors that get suckered. This rule applies to the biggest hedge funds and institutions that let their guard down and believe that they're getting a deal because they're special. If you don't believe me, why don't you ask the Hong Kong millionaires that bought complex debt instruments from Lehman Brothers or the Norwegian towns that bought subprime bonds from Citigroup?

When things go bad, Wall Street is happy to lean back on that "Risk Disclosure" statement you signed and collect their fees no matter what.

The way to avoid getting burned is a simple rule of thumb: *Try not to do business with anyone that has any kind of conflict of interest in regards to your money.* If they are getting paid a commission for selling you a tax-shelter product or annuity, they are out for themselves and their decisions are being driven more by fees than what's best for you. You can ignore this rule at your peril but I've seen the underbelly of the investing world and there will come a time when that conflict of interest will cost you money.

If you have a financial advisor who is being paid by the products he sells to you, there will be a moment where he'll rationalize a decision and convince himself that it's in your best interest. Better to never put your money manager in that position.

It's better yet to only deal with situations and people where your interests are aligned with their incentives. It all comes down to what is going to drive their behavior and you want to stay away from any situation where what's best for you isn't necessarily what's best for them.

Think of all sellers of financial products as vendors of any other product. Kick the tires, pit them against each other and always be ready to walk away. The moment you start salivating over a financial product is the moment you should consider whether you're the sucker at the poker table.

And in situations where the conflict is absolutely unavoidable, like when buying real estate and the agent represents both sides of the transaction, you have to go with people that have a track record of character and that have a long-term incentive for ethical behavior. When I drive around with the longtime friend of my father who has owned a local real estate agency for decades, I know that he has an incentive to find a good price for me and the seller, because his long-term business is in getting return customers and deal flow, not making an extra couple percent on any one transaction. You can still get cheated by someone you've known your whole life, so go into every situation with a skeptical eye and a handle on all the parties' incentives.

Q: My brother is a research doctor at the University of Chicago and he's working on a clinical trial for a drug company. I know the insider trading rules say that someone with fiduciary responsibility to the company can't trade on insider info, but since he's essentially a contract worker, can I trade the pharma company's stock based on what he tells me?

A: Here's my rule for any question related to insider trading and everything trading-wise: *If you have to ask if it's illegal, don't do it.* It's that simple. Don't ever do anything when trading that requires an opinion from a criminal lawyer beforehand. Now as to the specifics of your question, your brother definitely signed something saying he wouldn't share the results of that trial with anyone other than the company, so he is breaching his responsibility.

The pharmaceutical company has a reasonable expectation that its intellectual property and trade secrets won't leak out. That's the same for any employee of any company; you can't ask them to betray their employer or make money if they tell you something they shouldn't. And if you're not sure it's okay to hear what you're hearing, better just to not listen.

Even if you brother didn't sign anything, you should hold yourself to a higher standard than what any government requires of you.

Ask yourself, would you want your name on the cover of the Wall Street Journal in connection with buying this stock? If you have nothing to be ashamed or afraid of, go forth. In my career, I've had a few corporate insiders try to feed me privileged information; I turn and walk the other way and generally don't engage them ever again.

Plus you never really know why someone is bequeathing information on you, and it doesn't pay to find out if you're the patsy. And don't be a gossip hound who feels special because they know something others don't and leak information to a blogger.

Leave rumor mongering to the old ladies and get back to studying the company's fundamentals. Never straddle that ethical fence; sooner or later you'll fall over.

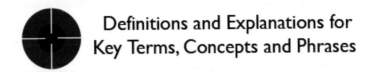

Definitions and Explanations for Key Terms, Concepts and Phrases

Bear –

Someone who believes the market or a stock is in a downward trend.

Bull –

Someone who believes the market or a stock is in a upward trend.

Call –

An option contract giving the owner the right (but not the obligation) to buy a specified amount of an underlying security at a specified price within a specified time. A call becomes more valuable as the price of the underlying asset appreciates.

For example, buying 1 call FB $30 January 2013 option gives me the right to buy 100 shares of Facebook on the third Friday of January of next year for $30 a share, no matter where FB is trading at that time. So if the stock is up above $30 a share, say at $40 a share, then the call would be worth at least $10. That would mean that a $300 investment in an FB call option would be worth $1000 if FB is at $40 by the third week of January. And if the stock goes up a bunch before then, obviously, I could sell the call option to someone else for big gains before next January if I wanted to.

And of course, as with any options trade, I could lose every penny of my capital if the stock is below the strike price ($30 in this case) when the expiration date comes.

Common Stock –

A security that represents ownership in a corporation. Holders of common stock have the most rights when it comes to the operating life of the corporation (electing directors, voting on a sale), but the least in a bankruptcy proceeding. Also called "ordinary shares" and in short-hand, simply "common".

Contrarian -

Contrarian means going against the grain, looking at investing as an exercise in not following the masses. Contrarians get into trouble when they are contrarian for contrarian's sake, and ignore fundamental realties (eg. "catching a falling knife"). The biggest returns in investing come from buying when no one else is and selling when everyone is buying on margin. And here are five reasons to be a contrarian:

1. If you ever want to be something more than average, you have to do things that nobody else will do.
2. When I see everybody panic, it's almost always when prices are already down.
3. When people on TV used to explain to me in 2007 that the economy and real estate and everything was great, we were at the top.
4. Whenever my inbox and the comments on my blogs turn into utter hate and anger and disgust, my own portfolio usually bounces.
5. The markets like to fool the most amount of people it can the most amount of time it can, and you've got to not be "most people" if you're going to not be part of the fools.
6. Over time you hope that the bulls or bears will join you and the stock will run (or collapse). Being a contrarian pays off when the herd joins (then the trick is knowing when to get out!)

Cost Basis -

Most directly connected to tax treatment of a capital gain, cost basis is calculated as either the purchase price or the price at which an asset was "received" (ex. A gift, a distribution). For investing purposes it is the average price paid for a an equity position.

Dividend -

A distribution of a portion of a company's earnings, decided by the board of directors, to a class of its shareholders. Most often quoted in terms of the dollar amount each share receives (dividends per share), and paid quarterly. The dividend yield is the percentage that the annual payment represents in relation to a stock price. Dividends are most often cash but may be stock or property. Dividends are traditionally paid by companies when they figure the excess return they can generate by holding the cash is lower than returning the capital to shareholders. Occasionally companies will "juice" the dividend as a way to entice people to buy the stock.

Earnings Per Share -

The portion of a company's profit allocated to each outstanding share of common stock. Earnings per share serves as an indicator of a company's profitability.

Fundamental Analysis-

Anything where you examine the underlying business to determine what you think a stock is worth. Includes look at a company's revenues, cash flows, dividends, debt, intellectual property and management. Fundamental analysis also includes looking at multiples such as Enterpise Value to Earnings Before Interest, Taxation, Deduction and Ammoritization (EV/EBITDA). It also includes considering how macroeconomic factors like interest rates and foreign exchange movement will impact a business.

*I'll give you two examples of how I come up with my ideas for trades because there are two primary ways I do it. The Dollar Stores as a short idea is a "top down" idea, meaning that I looked at the industry from the top down and then I had my team drill down and gather a ton of research and analysis for any Dollar Stores-related play. In this specific example, the idea of shorting the Dollar Stores came to me when I couldn't believe that our rural town here in NM was about to get a bunch more new Dollar Discount Stores even though we already had a bunch here. I've seen the retail sector cycle play out many times and the key to trading/investing in retail is to catch these chains when they are in expansion mode and to sell them when they get to saturation mode.

So my brain started turning because I knew that these Dollar Stores stocks are all up 500-1000% in the last few years as they were in the perfect storm for them to grow — a massive consumer "trade-down" in looking to pay less as the unemployment rate skyrocketed and the average household net worth collapsed 40% just as these guys were getting into the cookie-cutter expansion mode. So my brain started telling me maybe we've got a great storm of our own here to try to catch the top of this classic retail sector cycle. So I sent my guys to work and started doing my analysis and holy cow — the more I worked on the set up, the more excited I got. So by the time I'd spoken to every retail analyst and money manager I know and they all, even the most bearish of them, thought my analysis made tons of sense but that they still thought these Dollar Stores are going to go through the roof from these levels, I started writing for you guys and picking the two best plays to bet against the Dollar Store boom. Now to be clear, I could still be wrong on this trade, but that is what we're here to find out.

Another example of fundamental analysis I'll give you is called "bottom up" analysis and I used it when buying Apple back in the spring of 2003. After spending years analyzing stocks, I've memorized a lot of company's balance sheets and earnings multiples and things like that. I knew that Apple had a huge pile of cash in the bank, $8 per share to be exact at the time. And I have thousands of stock tickers blinking in front of me and I saw Apple drop 10% or so two or three days in a row as rumors circulated around the tech world that Apple was going to be buying Warner Music Group. I thought that sounded absolutely nuts and so I called around to my Apple sources (which at the time were MUCH more forthcoming with what the company was about to do) and they also thought that sounded absolutely nuts.

So when Apple got to $7 a share — meaning that I was buying the company essentially for free and that any future earnings would simply be gravy...I started buying Apple. As the company rolled out the iPod and its other iOS platforms soon thereafter, I saw the potential for Apple to change the way we were consuming music and I started telling my subscribers that within a couple years that Apple would be the world's largest music retailer. At the time, they had less than 5% of the market. They were indeed the world's largest music retailer just a couple years later. And as Steve Jobs started rolling out better and more functional iPods, I started telling everybody that the company would in a couple years start selling "iMiniMacBookPros For Your Pocket" — the iPhone as it turned out. So I stuck with my Apple because my "bottom up" analysis, meaning I found the stock individually based on analysis for it and it alone, and not necessarily for the entire sector. "Top Down" means you start with a sector or an economic concept and then drill down. "Bottom Up" means you start with an individual company and then move up to analyze its place in that sector and the broader economy. I use both Top Down and Bottom Up all the time.

(Editor's note: Reprinted from page 4 for reader's convenience.)

"Flip It" –

A concept that I created when I was learning to invest that is all about looking at the news, the trades, the analysis, and everything else completely upside down from what you've been taught. For example, when the economy is rosy, and everybody thinks it's a no-brainer to be long stocks, the markets will always be at highs — you want to Flip It and sell. When the economy sucks and everybody thinks it's nuts to invest in stocks, the market will be always be at lows — you want to Flip It and buy. It's loosely affiliated with the term "Contrarian".

Guidance –

Information that a company provides analysts and the public as its internal prediction of future earnings. When a company "guides up" or "guides down," it is revising the previous quarter's (or year's) estimates.

Hedging –

Hedging is taking some position that isn't part of your core holding but related to it, so even if you're wrong you'll at least make money on your hedge. Since you can choose when you put on positions and how big they'll be, you can hedge a position for a while and then take it off and be "unhedged".

*You'll cut into your potential gains if you spend money on "hedging" those positions, but as one of my mentors used to say, "May you lose money on all your hedges" because that usually means you're making big money on your actual investments/bets. Anyway, if you're worried that you're too heavily long both common and calls heading into the earnings reports and you want to hedge, I would suggest a pure hedge of buying some near-term slightly-out-of-the-money puts. I'd probably look at buying about enough of the puts to cover at least the common stock portion of your longs and then your calls still let you catch the upside of any major near-term rally in the underlying stock (and they'll even open you up to some positive gamma but let's not get distracted with Greek terms here). You could also look at shorting some calls with different times and strikes than the ones you currently are long to create different hedging strategies within each position, but I tend to think that most traders who do that stuff end up spending more time and energy and commissions and slippage than makes it worth it. Finally, you could find a stock that you think you could "pair" with each of your stocks, meaning that you short a similar stock to, say, F (in F's case you could consider GM a potential "paired" hedge), and hope that the rally in the stock you are long far outpaces the rally in the stock you are short as its pair.

(Editor's note: Reprinted from page 30 for reader's convenience.)

Long –

Taking a position in a security such that one benefits from price appreciation. "Getting long" a stock simply means buying it. Long is used colloquially for sectors and trends such as "I'm long biopharma" or "I'm long cloud computing."

Mr. Market –

Mr. Market is how Benjamin Graham explained the bi-polar nature of the market and how you should take advantage of it. Mr. Market is your business partner, and together you co-own the stock your investing in. Some days Mr. Market comes to work and is euphoric and wants to pay an absurd price for the part of the stock you own. Other days he shows up depressed and is willing to sell you his shares at a reduced price. Graham said that you need to use and abuse Mr. Market, buy when he thinks the world is going to end, sell when he thinks nothing bad will ever happen. This is different than being guided by what Mr. Market is feeling on any given day, you want to track the underlying business (the stock you own) not the whims of your unstable business partner!

Option –

Options give you the right to buy or sell typically 100 shares of a certain stock at a given price at a given date.

Pair Trade –

A strategy where you go long one stock and short a related stock, usually done with two companies that are competitors or in the same sector. By going long-short you are betting on how the two stocks perform in relation to each other, rather than movements in the overall market.

Parabolic –

"Parabolic" according to the standard dictionary is defined as "Of or having the form of a parabola or paraboloid." A parabola is "A plane curve formed by the intersection of a right circular cone and a plane parallel to an element of the cone or by the locus of points equidistant from a fixed line and a fixed point not on the line." Here's a picture of a parabola:

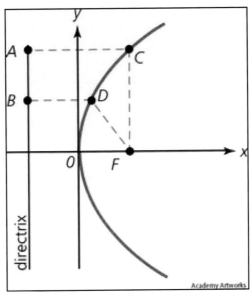

Now the way this all relates to a stock is that you should look at a stock chart and pretend that the intersection of the axis themselves are the start of the chart and you see that Apple's weekly stock chart looks a little bit "parabolic".

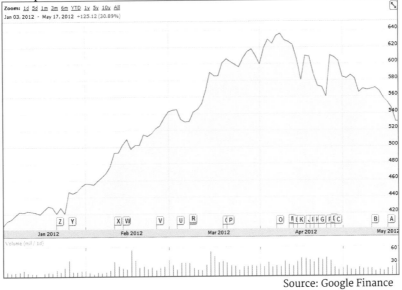

Source: Google Finance

At any rate, the main idea behind "parabolic moves" is that they are unsustainable because the stock has run up so much so fast that profit takers, shorts, bears, and worry warts are going to sell simply as a function of the stock having run up so much so fast, making it a self-fulfilling prophesy. I'm not a "technical analyst" or a "chartist" because I don't draw lines on stock charts to make my trading decisions, but common sense itself tells you that when Apple's gone from $380 to $540 in a few months' time, that people like you and me are going to do a little selling ourselves and that too can self-fulfill that prophesy.

Price-Earnings Ratio (P/E Ratio) –

A valuation ratio of a company's current share price compared to its per-share.

Calculated as: Market Value per Share / Earnings per Share (EPS).

Also sometimes known as "price multiple" or "earnings multiple". Generally a high P/E means that investors are "paying up" for a company's future earnings.

Put –

An option contract giving the owner the right, but not the obligation, to sell a specified amount of an underlying asset at a set price within a specified time. The buyer of a put option estimates that the underlying asset will drop below the exercise price before the expiration date.

Revolutionomics –

Those who empower, win. Those who protect, lose.

Believe it or not, that simple principle is all you need to know when it comes to investing in the trend to distribute the world's information and entertainment content on the Internet. The key is to buy companies when they are working to empower their user base and to sell them soon after they shift to protecting their own interests. You have seen the scenario played out repeatedly since Netscape first ushered the Internet revolution into the public markets more than a decade ago.

The endgame of the Internet is the total empowerment of the end user. Because the Internet has been built on open standards and the free flow of information, the 1.5bn people on this planet who have access to the web will continuously move to the places on the net that empower and liberate them the most. We users will constantly (and at an accelerated pace) move away from centres of control and toward self-empowerment.

And just as the tendency towards disorder in the universe cannot be controlled, nobody can stop the virtuous entropy of the internet revolution.

I have coined the term "revolutionomics" to describe this dynamic.

"Lock in," "switching costs" and many other similar strategies that the world's leading technology companies have built their business models on have no place in the end-user-powered networked world. Tech companies have long tried to lock their customers into proprietary standards, thus creating high switching costs for them. Control was yesterday's business model. The model that increasingly works on the Internet is to empower customers rather than control them.

Edward George Bulwer-Lytton, the English novelist and playwright, once wrote that the pen is mightier than the sword. That the Internet revolution will be fought using words, software and open networks – and on such a massive scale – is precisely why its impact will be much bigger than any revolution this world has gone through. Every revolution that has succeeded in the long term, including the American Revolution, has been about shifting power away from central control.

As the costs for technology development in this networked future continue to collapse, the only differentiator becomes one of execution and strategy. Only those companies that design their systems from the ground up to empower the end-user have any chance of long-term success.

Look no further than what is going on in the media industry for what happens to those who fight the virtuous entropy.

Years ago, I trademarked the term "They can't stop the revolution" as a catchphrase for the virtuous entropy of revolutionomics. And, indeed, that is exactly the point. Neither Yahoo, nor Apple, nor the music labels, nor the film studios can stop the empowerment of the individual.

Short or sell-short or "shorting a stock" –
Most people understand that shorting something means you'll make money if it goes down. Here's how it actually works: It's Saturday afternoon and you stop by your ex girlfriend's apartment to pick some of your old stuff. You guys are friends and all, so you just let yourself in. You're grabbing your clothes from behind the fridge and see that she's got a case of Budweiser sitting in the pantry next to it. You happen to be on your way to a pool party and you know that your frat boy friends will be out of beer by the time you make your "casually late" entrance. So you "borrow" that case of beer from your ex. That's called the locate, and since you didn't get her permission then that would be called doing it naked.

You get to the party and sure enough, your boyz are desperate for more beer, so you sell (read: short-sell, since it ain't your beer in the first place) them the case at a dollar a pop, and you just pocketed $24.

Sure enough, your ex calls you just then as she's got a new loser boyfriend who wants to drink some Bud and she wants to know why you've stolen her beer (naked shortsellers ALWAYS get in trouble).

The brilliant part of this particular trade is that you stop by the Safeway on your way to your ex's and pick up a case of bud for $15. And you've just "covered" your short sell at a nice $9 profit (you sold the beer at $24 and bought it back at $15, see?).

Then again, what happens if the state declares beer sales illegal before you get back to Safeway, so you end up having to buy the beer back at $40 a can, and that means you just spent $40/can X 24 cans = $960 to replace her beer. And since you only received $24 for the beer you sold at the party, you just lost $936 on your beer short sale. That's why shorting stock is so much more dangerous than buying stock -- you can lose unlimited amounts of money as the stock goes against you.

Spread –

1. The difference between what someone is willing to pay for a security and what someone is willing to sell that same security for. Often referred to in options trading, where the "bid-ask" (buy-sell) spread can be wide if that particular option is illiquid. The more liquid the market, the tighter the bid-ask spread will be.
2. The difference between yields in the bond market. You'll hear traders talk about the corporate bond spread, or what a company has to pay in interest rates above Treasuries.

Technical Analysis –

The analysis of past prices to forecast future prices. Often called "chart-reading". In technical analysis you don't look at the business fundamental of a company, you consider factors like volume, previous all-time highs and volatility to guide your investing. I don't use technical analysis because long-term I don't think capitalism rewards drawing lines on a chart, but you'll hear pundits and traders use different technical analysis terms. I've picked out some of the most popular you should be aware of.

Head and shoulders pattern–

When a security does the following:
1. Rises to a peak and subsequently declines.
2. Then, the price rises above the former peak and again declines.
3. And finally, rises again, but not to the second peak, and declines once more.

This is considered to be bearish. When a stock does the opposite, it is considered bullish.

HEAD AND SHOULDERS

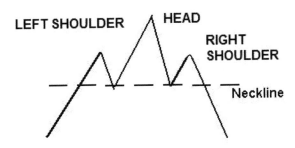

Resistance–

A price level that may prompt a net increase of selling activity.

Support–

A price level that may prompt a net increase of buying activity.

Breakout–

The concept whereby prices forcefully penetrate an area of prior support or resistance, usually, but not always, accompanied by an increase in volume.

Bollinger bands–

Bollinger Bands® consist of a center line and two price channels (bands) above and below it. The center line is an exponential moving average; the price channels are the standard deviations of the stock being studied. The bands will expand and contract as the price action of an issue becomes volatile (expansion) or becomes bound into a tight trading pattern (contraction).

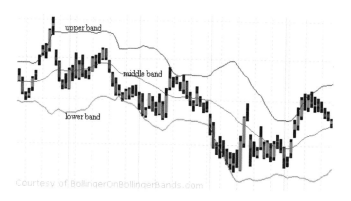

50 day moving average (50 DMA)–

Moving averages emphasize direction and the try to filter out extreme volume and price fluctuations. The point is to show a pattern and momentum of a longer term trend. 50 DMA is one of the most popular trends and stock movements are often talked about in terms of it (ie. 'The 30 DMA crossed the 50 DMA).

Value Investing –

Right off the bat let me say that all investing is value investing, no one seeks to systematically overpay for securities. That being said when you hear "Value Investing" it refers to teachings of Benjamin Graham, Warren Buffett's teacher and the first person to take investing from the dartboard to a respectable practice. His two books "Security Analysis" and "The Intelligent Investor" are still required reading on Wall Street. Graham espoused a strict system of what he called a "margin of safety," where you only ever buy a stock where if you're 100% wrong about the future, you'll still be O.K. Graham liked to invest in companies that were trading for as much cash as they had on the balance sheet, or for less than what they would fetch in a liquidation. The genius of Graham is that he taught investors to not think of stocks as just numbers moving up and down, but as a stake in an underlying business. Value investors look at stocks and ask "If I was going to buy 100% of this company, what price would I pay?" If the market cap is less than that answer, they buy.

VIX –

Short for the CBOE Volatility Index® and taken from their definition:

> "VIX measures market expectation of near term volatility conveyed by stock index option prices. Since volatility often signifies financial turmoil, VIX is often referred to as the 'investor fear gauge.' VIX is based on real-time option prices, which reflect investors' consensus view of future expected stock market volatility. During periods of financial stress, which are often accompanied by steep market declines, option prices – and VIX – tend to rise. The greater the fear, the higher the VIX level. As investor fear subsides, option prices tend to decline, which in turn causes VIX to decline. It is important to note, however, that past performance does not necessarily indicate future results."

I'll put it another way –– VIX is just one of many market signals and is way over-hyped in importance. Just because volatility is expected to go up, that doesn't mean stocks are about to go down. In fact traders could even be buying options betting on a sharp market rise and that would still push the VIX up! Use VIX to your contrarian advantage because most investors will just be scared when they see a big VIX number. Generally anything about 40 is a screaming buy signal for stocks and anything below 10 is a signal of complacency in the market.

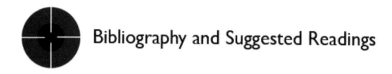

Bibliography and Suggested Readings

Altucher, James. *Trade like a Hedge Fund: 20 Successful Uncorrelated Strategies & Techniques to Winning Profits.* Hoboken, N.J.: Wiley, 2004.

Altucher, James. *Trade like Warren Buffett.* Hoboken, N.J.: Wiley, 2005.
Bernstein, Peter L. *Against the Gods: The Remarkable Story of Risk.* New York: John Wiley & Sons, 1996.

Beyer, Andrew. *Picking Winners: a Horseplayer's Guide.* Boston: Houghton Mifflin Co., 1994.

Buffett, Warren, and Lawrence A. Cunningham. *The Essays of Warren Buffett: Lessons for Corporate America.* New York: L. Cunningham, 2001.

Collins, James C., and Jerry I. Porras. *Built to Last: Successful Habits of Visionary Companies.* New York: HarperBusiness, 1994.

Cramer, Jim. *Confessions of a Street Addict.* New York: Simon & Schuster, 2002.

Dalla, Nolan, and Peter Alson. *One of a Kind: The Rise and Fall of Stuey "the Kid" Ungar, the World's Greatest Poker Player.* New York: Atria Books, 2005.

Das, Satyajit. *Traders, Guns & Money: Knowns and Unknowns in the Dazzling World of Derivatives.* Harlow, England: Financial Times Prentice Hall, 2006.

Einhorn, David. *Fooling Some of the People All of the Time: A Long Short Story.* Hoboken, N.J.: J. Wiley, 2008.

Fisher, Philip A. *Common Stocks and Uncommon Profits and Other Writings*. [Updated ed. New York: Wiley, 2003.

Garber, Peter M. *Famous First Bubbles: The Fundamentals of Early Manias*. Cambridge, Mass.: MIT Press, 2000.

Geisst, Charles R. *Wall Street: A History : From its Beginnings to the Fall of Enron*. [Rev. and expanded ed. Oxford: Oxford University Press, 2004.

Graham, Benjamin, David L. Dodd, Sidney Cottle, Roger F. Murray, and Frank E. Block. *Graham and Dodd's Security Analysis*. 5th ed. New York: McGraw-Hill, 1988.

Graham, Benjamin, and Jason Zweig. *The Intelligent Investor*. Rev. ed. New York: HarperBusiness Essentials, 2003.

Grant, James. *Mr. Market Miscalculates: The Bubble Years and Beyond*. Mount Jackson, VA: Axios Press, 2008.

Greenblatt, Joel. *You Can Be a Stock Market Genius: Uncover the Secret Hiding Places of Stock Market Profits*. New York: Simon & Schuster, 1999.

Katsenelson, Vitaliy N. *The Little Book of Sideways Markets: How to Make Money in Markets That Go Nowhere*. Hoboken, N.J.: Wiley, 2011.

Klarman, Seth A. *Margin of Safety: Risk-averse Value Investing Strategies for the Thoughtful Investor*. New York, N.Y.: HarperBusiness, 1991.

Lanyi, Andrew. *Confessions of a Stockbroker*. New York: Prentice Hall Press, 1992.

Lefevre, Edwin. *Reminiscences of a Stock Operator*. New York: J. Wiley, 1994.

Levitt, Steven D., and Stephen J. Dubner. *Freakonomics: A Rogue Economist Explores the Hidden Side of Everything*. Rev. and expanded ed. New York: William Morrow, 2006.

Lewis, Michael. *Liar's Poker: Rising Through the Wreckage on Wall Street*. New York: Norton, 1989.

Loehr, James E. *The Power of Story: Rewrite Your Destiny in Business and in Life*. New York: Free Press, 2007.

Lowenstein, Roger. *When Genius Failed: The Rise and Fall of Long-Term Capital Management*. New York: Random House, 2000.

Lowenstein, Roger. *The End of Wall Street*. New York: Penguin Press, 2010.

Malkiel, Burton Gordon. *A Random Walk Down Wall Street: The Time-tested Strategy for Successful Investing*. New York: W.W. Norton, 2003.

Matthews, Jeff. *Pilgrimage to Warren Buffett's Omaha a Hedge Fund Manager's Dispatches from Inside the Berkshire Hathaway Annual Meeting*. New York: McGraw-Hill, 2009.

McLean, Bethany, and Joseph Nocera. *All the Devils are Here: The Hidden History of the Financial Crisis*. New York: Portfolio/Penguin, 2010.

Mesquita, Bruce. *Predictioneer's Game: Using the Logic of Brazen Self-interest to See and Shape the Future*. New York: Random House, 2009.

Mezrich, Ben. *Bringing down the House: the Inside Story of Six MIT Students Who Took Vegas for Millions*. New York: Free Press, 2002.
Miller, Norman C. *The Great Salad Oil Swindle,*. New York: Coward McCann, 1965.

O'glove, Thornton L., and Robert Sobel. *Quality of Earnings: The Investor's Guide to How Much Money a Company is Really Making*. New York: Free Press, 1987.

Poundstone, William. *Fortune's Formula: the Untold Story of the Scientific Betting System that Beat the Casinos and Wall Street*. New York: Hill and Wang, 2005.

Reinhart, Carmen M., and Kenneth S. Rogoff. *This Time is Different: Eight Centuries of Financial Folly*. Princeton: Princeton University Press, 2009.

Richard, Christine S. *How Hedge Fund Manager Bill Ackman Called Wall Street's Bluff*. Hoboken: John Wiley & Sons, Inc., 2010.

Schilit, Howard Mark. *Financial Shenanigans*. 2nd ed. New York, N.Y.: McGraw-Hill, 2002.

Schwager, Jack D. *Market Wizards: Interviews with Top Traders*. New York, NY: HarperBusiness, 19931989.

Schwed, Fred. *Where are the Customers' Yachts ?, or, a Good Hard Look at Wall Street*. New York: Wiley, 1995.

Shapiro, Carl, and Hal R. Varian. *Information Rules: A Strategic Guide to the Network Economy*. Boston, Mass.: Harvard Business School Press, 1999.

Shefrin, Hersh. *Beyond Greed and Fear: Understanding Behavioral Finance and The Psychology of Investing*. Boston, Mass.: Harvard Business School Press, 2000.

Smith, Adam. *The Money Game,*. New York: Random House, 1968.

Smith, Adam. *Supermoney*. [1st ed. New York: Random House, 1972.

Soros, George. *The Alchemy of Finance: Reading the Mind of the Market*. New York: Simon and Schuster, 1987.

Staley, Kathryn F. *The Art of Short Selling*. New York: Wiley, 1997.

Swedroe, Larry E., and Jared Kizer. *The Only guide to Alternative Investments You'll Ever Need: The Good, The Flawed, The Bad, and the Ugly*. New York: Bloomberg Press, 2008.

Swensen, David F. *Unconventional Success: A Fundamental Approach to Personal Investment*. New York: Free Press, 2005.

Taleb, Nassim. *The Black Swan: The Impact of the Highly Improbable.* New York: Random House, 2007.

Train, John. *Money Masters of Our Time.* New York, N.Y.: HarperBusiness, 2000.

Whitman, Martin J., and Martin Shubik. *The Aggressive Conservative Investor.* New York: Random House, 1979.

Index

About the Author

Cody Willard is an American investor, television anchor and formerly the manager of a successful hedge fund. He is the founder of CL Willard Capital. Willard also serves as an adjunct professor at Seton Hall University where he teaches a class called "Revolutionomics" focused on technology and business and serves on Finance Committee of the University of New Mexico Alumni Board. He is the author of a subscription-based investment newsletter TradingWithCody.com and the author of The Cody Word on the Wall Street Journal's Digital Network.

He wrote a monthly investment column for The Financial Times and a trading diary for *TheStreet.com* and was the long-time featured tech investor and expert economist on CNBC's *Kudlow & Company.*

Cody's approach to the markets and his insights on trading and investing have been featured on *The Tonight Show with Jay Leno,* ABC's *20/20* and *Good Morning America, CBS Evening News,* CNBC's *SquawkBox,* Jon Stewart's *The Daily Show,* as well as in the *Financial Times, Wall Street Journal, New York Times,* and many other outlets.

He was an anchor on the *Fox Business Network,* where he was the co-host of the long-time #1-rated show on the network, *Fox Business Happy Hour.*

He began his career at Oppenheimer & Co. in 1996 (after his first job in New York City, a barista at Starbucks) and was Chief Analyst at Visual Radio, a technology venture capital fund, and vice president of wholesale operations at Broadview Networks, a telecommunications company.

He is a musician who has played backup guitar for Bob Weir, Neil Sedaka, Lorrie Morgan and others, and is a songwriter and producer with the indie rock band The Muddy Souls.

Contributor, **Ashwin Deshmukh**, is an active value investor and the manager of a pooled fund for several family offices. He specializes in commodity futures, equities and manages a grain merchandising firm. Ashwin has extensive real estate experience and oversees his family's U.S. and India property portfolio. He is a partner in PLAN Energy L.P., an energy partnership that seeks to develop natural gas wells in the Marcellus Shale formation; PLAN has brought three active wells on-line to date and participated in the leasing of 6000 acres. Ashwin holds a B.A. from New York University in mathematics and economics. He is the founder of crowdfunding startup based in New York City, where he lives. He may be reached anytime, day or night, via his twitter -- @ashwindeshmukh.

Contributor, **William Fox**, is the Chief Technology Officer for Willard Media Ventures. Previously, Bill was the Information Technology Manager at a financial services company in San Diego where he developed a proprietary software system for the company. He has worked as a technology manager in the financial industry for over 15 years and has over 25 years experience in information technology. Bill holds a B.S. degree in Computer Science from California State University, Chico.

Made in the USA
Lexington, KY
16 March 2014